To Sophia
of the bi
& bound
The wor
David Morgan

CW01637282

The River Was a God

David Lee Morgan

Stairwell Books

Published by Stairwell Books
70 Barbara Drive
Norwalk
CT 06851 USA

161 Lowther Street
York, YO31 7LZ

www.stairwellbooks.co.uk
@stairwellbooks

The River Was a God © 2018 David Lee Morgan and Stairwell Books

All rights reserved. No part of this publication may be reproduced, stored in or introduced into a retrieval system, or transmitted, in any form, or by any means (electronic, mechanical, photocopying, recording, e-book or otherwise) without the prior written permission of the author.

The moral rights of the author have been asserted.

ISBN: 978-1-939269-68-3

Printed and bound in the UK by Imprint Digital
Layout design: Alan Gillott
Cover image of David Lee Morgan by Chantal Guevara

"David's work is a lion's roar folded neatly into a snake bite and mailed to the Aristocracy of the world with a note saying 'Do not open 'til Election Day.'

"I've known David and his work for some time now and it never ceases to amaze. His themes are always current yet routed in history and experience. It's sometimes a slap across the face with a feathered glove or a musical note played and held constant, lifting you to lofty heights and then just as you reach the edge of the stratosphere it cuts, and leaves you cascading downward rushing past all the moments you just inhaled on the way up.

"He is hammer and tongue, passion and revolution, rebellion and nurture all in a single pen stroke."

Tshaka Campbell, poet and spoken word artist

"*The River Was a God* makes history dance in the page, the head and the heart. It is the product of hundreds of books and a careful dialogue between intellect and imagination, an un-ignorable contribution from one of the most important political poets in the field today."

Pete (the Temp) Bearder

"David isn't just a poet, he's a surgeon, using verse as a scalpel to dissect the human condition, taking it apart word by word, delving inwards to reveal God living in our very molecules, the same force that spins the planets relentlessly fights for mortal breath."

Clare Ferguson-Walker, poet and artist

"David Lee Morgan echoes the howl of Ginsberg, mixing Shelley's passion for humanity with the revolutionary spirit of Che Guevara. I kid you not. David's poetry is, like the man, a force for change."

Matt Panesh (aka monkey poet),
President, UK Centre, International Theatre Institute

"About bloody time. Finally the release of a much awaited collection of works by one of the most expressive poets on the spoken word circuit."

Salam Jones, writer

"David Lee Morgan is one of the only true revolutionary poets we have left in the west. These words will propel you from the very seed of our communal existence into a future we can barely imagine. David's work is controversial, it's provocative, while being astoundingly beautiful – everything poetry should be. And there's a generation of poets who learnt the trade through this trilogy."

Lisa Luxx, poet, essayist and activist

"*The River Was a God* has been truly captivating, from the very first poem and onwards. I hope it has a wide reach, it deserves it. Through David Lee Morgan's poetry, the revolution is not just a thing of the imagination, he renders it real and tangible; a fair and just world that is on its way. And it starts with you."

JJ Bola Writer, poet, author of No Place to Call Home

"David Lee Morgan is a poet/spoken word artist, whose brilliantly crafted thought-provoking, powerful and inspiring work pushes us as the audience to reflect on the life we are in. *The River Was a God* is a book in kind to David's performances; I can hear and see him in action as I read each word of every poem."

Nat Nye the Lyrical Alchemist

"David Lee Morgan... You can hear his voice in his written words, words that hold a quality of spice and youthful talent at ease. His structures come from the wisdom of one who knows not all knowledge is in the tell but the telling, too. He uses frank honesty to make you feel what losing love and gaining wisdom feels like. He teaches. He teaches the history of his beliefs and the transformation from one state of people's revolution to another, what was lost and what was gained. With his societal politics he takes you to the future of a communist revolution, worldwide and still deeply personal, where truths are stranger than our everyday, easily understood fictions. The Morgan is a real life charter of life who brings all that to his poems, plays and shows. Enjoy that which is within... It's a trip."

Jah-Mir Early, improv poet

"His writing is ambitious, complex with visceral imaginings of the world around us, triggering autonomic responses compelling us to join a revolution, the revolution – any revolution that will result in a fearless dismantling of imperialist constructs. Yet not without hope, his vision is of a world where we all fit, where justice is the very air we breathe, and this is what will keep the reader reading and evolving."

Nairobi Thompson, writer, poet and
Publishing Director – Nubian Jak Community Trust

"I like David both for his wonderful poetry and his radical political views. He is simply an important poet of this turbulent world. He screams out very often loudly, poignantly… as if these verses are set to shake many capitals around the world, but again he appears as subtle, as ambiguous."

T M Ahmed Kaysher, poet, essayist and director of the Saudha Society of Poetry and Indian Music

"David Lee Morgan's writing could not be more incendiary if it was written on blue touch-paper. From the precision-crafted dialectics of *Science, Love and Revolution*, where I first encountered his work, to the psycho-spiritual philosophic enquiry of *Building God*, to the razor-sharp dystopian science fiction of *The Other Side of the Flood*, Morgan maintains a peerless revolutionary spirit of analysis and enquiry. He roots his impassioned and often devastating ideas and theses in classical storytelling and drama as much as the shock and awe of the spoken word.

"There are quite literally no other writers working today in the nebulous and ill-defined, often solipsistic and shallow field of spoken word poetry with a comparable rigour, depth and commitment in their writing. Flying in the face of the fetishised aesthetic of 'direct lived experience' – so often simulated and appropriated by lesser writers – his poems address a public and universal 'we'; a bold artistic choice in an era of tightly-focused and divisive identity politics.

"David Lee Morgan is not just a writer, and these are not just stage shows, or a poetry collection – *The River Was a God* is part pantheistic manifesto, part monstrous prophecy and part searing counterculture doctrine. His verses are expressed with a grace and flow that reveals his musical background and knowledge of the poet's craft. It is an essential publication in an era of throwaway tracts and pamphlets. Read it, share it, nail it to the door of your church."

Bram E. Gieben aka Texture, Black Lantern Music

To my wonderful sisters and brothers,

Rob, Anne, Bri and Joli

The River Was a God

Science, Love and Revolution

Word

It is written
In the beginning was the word
But I think
In the beginning was the tiger

I had a dream where the tiger and I stood side by side
And the air was alive with the music of our beating hearts
This is my tiger, I said. Isn't she beautiful
Her teeth cut like diamonds, but they shine like stars
Then the tiger purred, the purr became a growl
The growl became a word, the time to dance is… now!

[*roar, primate animal sounds*]

HAND

hunh, ha, hey, ho
eh, ih, ah, ew
eee, ay, iy, oh

TOOL

pah, buh, duh,
tig, ga, nuh,
kuh, juh, le,
suh, muh , chuh
r-r-r-r-r-ragh, zuh, vuh

FIRE

[*laughter*]

WORD

mother banana berry beetle grub yam
sister uncle brother father cousin kin clan
impala monkey cheetah catfish
bow and arrow hook and line
hunger death desire
dance dream moon wind
wolf enemy dog friend
animal-fur obsidian sea-shell
river lake ocean, barter boat wheel
sickle dam plough, millet rice maize
water-canal
goat horse cattle cow, priest king city wall
prison slave wife, road army empire
ritual sacrifice

planet alphabet tablet scroll
number circle triangle star
festival temple diamond gold
paper money poetry war
castle kingdom pilgrim pope
nativity communion jihad hijra
lord and lady serf and outlaw
carnival cathedral catapult crusade
compass telescope sextant astrolabe
buccaneer sugar-cane cotton-gin slave-trade
printing-press protest guillotine barricade

factory foundry model-t monopoly
gasoline caffeine telephone saxophone
black-hole rockn'roll blue-suede free-trade
concrete wall-street war-crime picket-line
colony corporation contraception insurrection

hospital popsicle methadone chromosome
pizzeria gonorrhea nagasaki hiroshima
penicillin television auschwitz crucifix

lipstick dayshift weblog gulag hot-dog kalashnikov
microchip paperclip spaceship cheese dip

blood brain demon idea
mud angel reason ikea
love anger grief absolution
vaccination air-pollution
education evolution
inspiration revolution

danger freedom
building breeding
without a *we are*, there is no *i am*
the river was a god until we built a dam

EGYPT

Growing up out of the river
Out of the dark brown mud of an African rain
Growing up out of the river
Swimming in the centuries
Black Athena of the ancient world
Dancing in the triangle and the square
Pythagoras and astronomy
Moses and Deuteronomy
Papyrus and the hieroglyph
Tempting Plato to leave his cave
And question the universe
Swept over by the Hyksos,
Romans and Mohammedans
Christians and Napoleons, British
And the never ending battle
Of wind and river, sand and mud
Mother of the Mediterranean
The Red Sea, and the Aegean,
Bowed down under the centuries
The brown top of Africa
Surrounded by a new black mud
That is drowning Arabia in a sea of blood
And the wind beings rise up
Desert wind sweeping the continents
Shivering the spider web world of
Sky and Fox, BBC, Al Jazeera
Listen to the children
Growing up out of the river
Where the Nile delta sings
In the cotton field spring
In the spinning wheel whine
In the factory roar
In the millions who pour into Tahrir square

Chanting *“Baoo demana we Baoo Kalaweena”*
You have stolen our blood and kidneys
“We Bneshhat Ehna we Ahaleena”
Now we are the starving, we and our families
You have given our land to strangers
You have traded in lies and torture
You have dined on blood and murder
You live in palaces
Drive by us in limousines
Fly over us in jets
Rule over us as if we were nothing but slaves
Now we rise up from the grave
And you will do anything to stop us
Ballot boxes stuffed full of corpses
Rape and religion wedded to make monsters
And yes, you can kill us in millions
But how will you live then
Who will feed you
Who will dig your wells of water and oil
Who will build your chariots and palaces
Who will build your magnificent tombs
You will never defeat us
We carry the earth on our backs
We open our mouths and speak in flame
We lift up our eyes and see it is you who are afraid
We will bury you
And your bones will nourish our dreams

BULLET

(London, August 2011)

Bang! out of the barrel of a gun I sped
Into the body of a black man
Into the body of a black
BOY BOY BOY
Assume the position
Spread'em wide
In front of your girl friend
In front of your mother
In front of your daughter and son
Put you in prison, yes, and I kill plenty
But even better, I make you into your own death penalty
I am the *War On Terror*. You are the enemy within
Man or woman, high or low.
Don't bother to show me your diploma
It's there on your skin

You are the flame of resistance
That I can never quite extinguish
You are the angry fire
That I fear more than truth
And I am the definition of liar
You are the light that blazed up in Tottenham
And a hundred other places, so bright
It could be seen across the Mediterranean
I am the darkness waiting
You are the stand-up-straight of a new generation.
You are the broken glass and torn up pavement
You are the golden beach beneath, if only you can find it
I am the man on the TV calling you mindless

I watch you

Change into every color and race
Communicate in ways I can't keep up with
Be brave a thousand times in every hour
But look around – I still have power

I am the bullet and the gun. I am the serpent tongue
I move armies, empty bellies, turn bones to dust
I am a treasure chest of fantasy, pleasure and shame
I have access to your brain more often than you do
I'm running with you on your feet, it's my arm too
That torched your neighbour's shop, my fingers you
Must free from an iron grip around your thoughts
Kettling you, ghetto-ing you, four long days and nights
Letting you burn the wrong places, keeping you out of the right
Revolution is a hurricane and the wind blows wildly
When young lions roar in pain and strike out blindly
Jackals hide in the tall grass waiting their chance
Until you learn to fight with wisdom, I rule the dance

DUH-MOCKRACY

Back in the Middle Ages
They had this thing called
The Church
And it was their gig to tell you God's will and what to do about it
Then Martin Luther hit the nail on the head and said
You decide
But that was too simple and way too dangerous
So they backed off, made a few changes
And come up with this thing called
        Duh-mockracy!
Who decides
        Duh-mockracy!
Where God is the man with the TV stations
God is the man with the guns to take'em
God is the man with the money to buy the guns
To take the stations to con-vince the nation
That he is the suppository of divine revelation
Who decides
        Well, we all took a vote and I voted against it, but…
Who decides
        Well, I don't like it but there's nothin' I can do about it…
Who put the lines on the maps that make the corpses fall on one side
while the other side plays
        Duh-mockracy!
Who drew the lines around Palestine
Who dug a ditch around an oil field and called it Kuwait
They say there are no pacifists in gasoline lines, but
When the majority votes for national salvation
When the majority votes for mass incineration
When the majority votes for racial purification
Fuck'em

The Age of Enlightenment

Je m'appelle Denis Diderot

They sentenced me to twenty-one years
Of frequent hunger and constant hard work
I thanked the judges and rolled up my sleeves
We were building a dictionary of the world
Covering everything related to human curiosity
So naturally we began sniffing at the asshole of the universe
Where the most beautiful flowers grow in shit
The sweet smell of stink, the love of calluses, rough hands
Dumb pleasures, howls of pain, life hungry death
Filth and excess, the word made flesh, and yet
Glowing inside, like a morning sunrise –
The rational mind

We collected everything, studied the work of every hand, documented every skill, engaged the great minds of our continent, cast it all into movable type, fired up printing presses day and night, shipped out books by the wagon load, trailing mule shit and wheel ruts, crossing mountains, dodging floods. We were an industry of the mind, making a new kind of property, selling it to all kinds of people – not only priests and scholars – they drank us down in the tea and coffee houses, and when they opened their mouths, our words came out, but in a new blend, with the flavour of each new mind, and it bubbled over into the streets and alleys, palaces and dives, even just talking was intoxicating, as we all drank down the spirit of the times.

How could we be to blame for the holocaust to come, when we were fighting for the magic of the mind's wonders, for the freedom to ask any question? We were not an infection, not fanatics – we were the enemy of everything dogmatic – and revolution was not a religion, it was a clap of thunder, it was a prison break over the crumbling walls of a dying empire out into the wide open space. We were the liberators of the human race. How could we be to blame for napalm and the atom bomb, slavery, genocide, and a planet ripped wide open and gutted for profit and plunder.

TIME OUT FOR DIALECTICS

We live in a metaphysical age
Physical, because even the invisible is material
Matter in motion, an infinite ocean of repetition and change
Meta-physical, because we never see it the way it is
We see it the way we make it to be
Which isn't to say it's make-believe
It's make-happen
And the happening is how we see
Until it becomes a habit and then it becomes how we don't see
Don't see the new
Don't even see the possibility of the new
But one divides into two
That's dialectics

For example…
Metaphysics says – the chair is there
I know it's there, because when I sit on it
(sits on chair)
My ass doesn't hit the floor
Metaphysics says – the chair is there
Dialectics says – yes it is there
On the other hand
(kicks chair across stage)
No it isn't

Everything divides into two because everything is coming and going
Atoms, electrons, ideas, emotions
Never entirely here or there but always kind of on the way

We look out at the world and see objects floating in space
But there is no truly empty space and no absolutely indivisible objects
Everything is process, movement and storm
One divides into two
The old and the new
The dying away and the fighting to be born
That's dialectics

BACK TO THE ENLIGHTENMENT

We were born into a world of circles, tied up in tradition, bowed down in obligation to those who stood outside, above our circle, who were only ever in a higher circle. I bow to you, you bow to him, he bows to the lord, the lord bows to the king, and we all bow down to god or the devil, it doesn't really matter which, because even hell is in circles.

And in a world like this, property was kind of democratic
Because it wasn't truly property until it could be taken away
By anybody – from anybody – the democracy of money

Property was individuality
Property broke down borders
Property was the atomic one
Multiplied by infinity
Property was possibility
Without property, there is no trade
No travel from country to country
Without property, there is no geography

And when we found we could turn the products of the mind into property
Peasants who played violin for the lord and lady's pleasure
Became composers, makers of sheets of music that could be bought and sold
Even ideas became a new kind of gold
And what could you buy with it?

Freedom
The freedom of things
In the marketplace of ideas

There are those who argue
That true science and philosophy
Began with money
That the idea of a universal substance
Wasn't simply dreamed up
It was invented
Money became a fact
Then it became an idea
Only then did we ask
If anything can be measured in money
What is it that money measures

And so it began
The search for a universal glue
That would bind us together
But one divides into two
And if money is the measure
It must also be true
That anything can be broken into pieces
And counted
As property

Books
Property
Ideas
Property
Cows
Property
Loaves of bread
Property
Men
Property
Women
Property

We should have known
If anything can be measured in money
Property isn't ownership
It's being owned

Beast Market

(*Capital*, by Karl Marx, chapters 1-4)

If I were alive
I would be your greatest lover
I would build you cities, feed your children
Fill up your lives with music and dancing
I would cover the earth with wheat fields and rice paddies
Drill down into its core to pull out strings of steel and oil
I would scrape the sky with desert sand melted into glass
Cool the hot, heat the cold, charm the fish out of the oceans
And teach the trees to stand in a row and rain down manna
I would multiply you

If I were alive
I would teach you the meaning of hell
I would blast you with war
Rip your children from your arms
Swallow them in famine
Smother them into silence
Dry up their tears with death
I would teach you to fear your neighbor
Train you to march in step

You might even come to believe in me
Isn't this how a wounded god would love?
With kindness and gifts, wonderful gifts
Mixed in with pieces of heartless cruelty
And if my cruelty is on a global scale
So are my gifts

And the greatest gift of all, I would do this through you
How else could it be? You made me. Now I make you
I am the law of value

The profit and loss ledger of the earth
I was born in the gulf between what you can do
And what you are worth
And look around
You can do miracles
But what are you worth…
How much do you eat
Do you live in a house or on the street
What does it take to make and replace you
That much, no one can take away from you
And still have you
But after that, everything is fair game
After that, it becomes worthwhile to own a slave
After that, the more you make, the more there is to steal
Until you, who produce the food, become the meal
And the wonders you have made
Become a curse, become a plague
Become a gang of howling wolves
But somehow they are riding in sleighs
And it's you pulling at the traces
And the whip cracks – that's me – I am the whip
But the wolves imagine they are in control and they
Snarl and slash at each other as they drive you forward
And you do go forward
So what if you leave behind a trail of blood

I am the hurricane that blows you through life
The profit drive, the whip of the world
I am measured in money but I am not money
I am in every good that goes to market but I am not physical
I am in every tool but I am not useful
I am you, your sweat, your time, your mind
Stolen away from you and congealed into a ghost
Not an evil spirit but an abstract principle
Coded into the grooves of habit and material
I weigh the world and say what is valuable
What counts
And it happens

Over an almost infinite number of individual transactions
I swallow and digest every exception, I break all regulation
I am the price of everything, I am the universal religion
I am the law
I am god
Kill me
Or I will own you forever

CRAZY SANTAS OCCUPY THE WORLD

This poem comes with a story – about the guy who had the biggest influence on me becoming a revolutionary communist: Santa Claus. In particular, it's about my memory of one movie: Miracle on 34th Street, the original version with John Payne, Maureen O'Hara, Natalie Wood as the little girl, and Edmund Gwenn as Santa.

In this movie, Santa Claus – THE REAL SANTA – has come to New York and for some reason has taken a job at Macy's as the department store Santa. And there's a scene where Santa is sitting on his... throne, I guess you'd call it, and boys and girls are coming up and sitting on his lap and telling him what they want for Christmas. And we can see that next in line is a little girl and her mother – as we think – who is anxious to talk to Santa first.

So she rushes up to him and says, "Listen, I'm not her real mother, I'm only her foster mother. Her real mother and father were murdered by the Nazis in Amsterdam, and she just got here, and she doesn't speak a word of English, only Dutch. And I've tried to explain to her that you won't understand what she's saying, but she says, 'No, no, no, you don't understand. Santa Claus is for every little boy and girl in the world – and I'm a little girl, so of course he'll understand me.' And I don't know what to say: she's already had her heart broken once... "

Now if this had been real life, the guy probably would have said, "Jeez, I don't know. Buy her a present. Buy her three. Here's a catalogue." But it isn't real life, it's a Hollywood movie, and in this movie, it's THE REAL SANTA. So he says to the mother, "Don't worry." Then he turns to the little girl and says...

Well, I don't know what he says, because it's in Dutch. And her eyes light up and she comes running and jumps in his lap, and they start jabbering away in Dutch and they sing a song about Sinterklaas. When I first saw this movie, I didn't know anything about the real world – I was the same age as the little girl – but I knew that was the way it should be, that wherever you travelled, no matter how long and hard the journey, especially if it was a long, hard journey, the first words you should hear when you get there are, "Welcome Home."

Crazy Santas

Imagine you were this cool old guy who loved children
Truly and deeply
Loved every beat of the way they stiff little tick-tock walk, and the monkey talk, and the roar of the buzz of the whisper of the butterfly why of honey and wonder and thirsty hunger. They give you their hand with everything in it, and your heart lurches into... Give me a place to stand and I will move the universe, squeeze it down into the perfect toy to light the smile inside your eye (I)... would give you anything. Imagine this, multiplied by every newborn smile in a heartbreak world – if you could be *Santa* for every boy and girl. Imagine a magic workshop powered by twinkle of the eye drive, quantum indecision, and reindeer jive, every elf in all eleven dimensions, drugged and demented, but working with manic precision, a just-in-the-nick-of-time engine (that's why they call you Saint Nick), and in the back of the sleigh a bag big enough to carry its weight in wishes. This is it! the delicious impossible minute when every child on the planet is given the

one perfect gift that says this is your world – and you belong in it
Imagine you could do this one wonderful thing
But for the rest of the year that was all you could do
And the toys would go out and be used up and worn out and broken
And that was good, the way it should be, that was why you would build them
Toys were made to be broken, not children
But in the war-torn days of the in-between year, the names would change but it was always King Herod's reign, and his soldiers would go from door to door with bloody swords, while you all worked on through tears and horror, knowing you could never make it right, no matter how magical that one perfect night
What would you do?
Would you go on working
When you could only give the one magic minute
Better than nothing, and who could argue with arithmetic
Or would you go crazy with the weight of anger and grief
Would you feel responsible, would you feel like a thief
Living a life so sweet, full of hard work done well
When so many children are living in hell
Some people can't ever get enough
Give them a minute and they want eternity, the kind who can never be happy with even a scrap of cruelty, they go crazy at the thought of one child dying a needless death, they can't rest, they've gotta be moving, doing, making more than a difference, making EVERYTHING different
These are the Crazy Santas who never give up
Crazy Santas mad with love
Crazy Santas get up at the crack of dawn, work boots on, march out onto the field, into the street, get beat, fight back, get shot at, don't stop, live life hot-wired
Crazy Santas are dangerous, but it's a dangerous world
Some people can't help fighting back
Whenever they see the weak attacked
They live like champions

In the army of the never-had-a-chance
Some of them pick up the gun
Some of them live like saints
All of them are powered by love
All of them make mistakes
Some say we need more magic minutes, that's the best we can do
But I believe we need to reach out for eternity, we need to be
Crazy Santas who never give up
Crazy Santas mad with love

Samson

Did you ever wish you could be like Samson
Hair grown long again
Big and strong again
Between the pillars of
Right and wrong again
One mighty shove and then
Bring it all tumbling down
The end of a nightmare world
Where baby girls are put to death
For the crime of being the wrong sex
Where girls and boys are given guns instead of toys
And made to fight and die for the light
That's stolen from their eyes, cut to fit
And pasted on a Wall Street bankers diamond tie clip
Yeah, maybe the whip and the African slave ship
Have been replaced by the ticker tape and the microchip
And the factory sweatshop has sprouted legs
And learned to walk across borders
But every new world order it's the same old song
Where the rich have rights and the poor get wronged
And the chairman of the board and the drug lord
And the gun dealer and the born again politician faith healer
They're all singing in the same choir
Swinging and swaying at the same club
You get baptized in fire
They get their sins washed away
In oil and money and blood
Did you ever feel like Noah before the flood
Praying for the day some vengeful god
Would say – I've had enough
And wash those bastards away
Did you ever feel like Hercules
Sent out to slay the many headed beast

But every time you chop off one head
Whack!
Two more grow back
Did you ever feel like you had so much love locked up inside
But you couldn't let it out, couldn't let it go
Had to keep hold of an icy cold silence
Or you might explode in mindless, raging violence

Living in a Marvel Comic Book strip
Knowing that the planet's in a death grip
Looking for a power that can shake it
Looking for a weapon that can break it
Look at all the love you got inside you
Let it be the fire that ignites you
Living in a world of violence
But the power is love and the weapon is…

Science…
Is dangerous, and it
Brings on changes, and it
Opens up possibilities
Even the ground beneath our feet is
Not so solid, not so safe
They burned scientists at the stake
'Cause they were afraid of the trouble we'd make
And you know what? They were right
We can make day from night
We can turn darkness into light
And the power that reaches out to the stars
And into the atom and back in time
Can turn on a dime
And look at the lock on the prison bars
That keep us caged
It's a power that grows from age to age
From the work of the hand and the work of the brain
We think and we do and we dream and we make
And we learn from the lesson of every mistake
And all our achievements and all that is known

Are built on the bones of what's come before
It's true of the study of stones, stars, biology and human society

So when the powers that be sneer at our history
At our victory and defeat in the laboratory of the street
They not only steal from the living, they rob the dead
Of all they fought and bled and died for
From the back alleys of Paris to the storming of the Winter Palace
From the cane fields of Haiti to the Vietnam rice paddy
From Tiananmen to Tahrir Square
From Malcolm to Marx, Mau Mau to Chairman Mao
These are our bones, our stepping stones to tomorrow
And the modern day vampires try to suck out the marrow
Of knowledge and vision and the courage that comes with them
But you who are fighting for a world that's not bought and sold
Where only in the human heart do you find the truest gold
You must be warriors with heads that are old
With wisdom and young with fire
Oh my sisters, oh my brothers
Don't believe the liars

What Is To Be Done

The revolution will not come until it has pierced your heart

Until every cruelty and injustice
No matter who it is done to
Feels as if it were done to you
Until you are naked, open wide
Wounded by every homeless cry
A mother to every hungry child
A native son to every tribe
Stranded in the forest flame
Swallowing smoke and tears of rage
Running from the thunder of a helicopter gun
The revolution will not come

Until your back aches
And the sun bakes you
And the pain breaks you
Until every minute of your life hurts
And the ripe fruit falls down into the dirt
Because your fingers and your bones and your brain are numb
The revolution will not come

Until every cop car is looking for you
For what you are, not what you do
And you stand on the earth, branded
By the wrong accent, the wrong colour skin
The wrong sexuality, the wrong mother tongue
Too fat, too thin, too old, too young
The revolution will not come

Until you walk the street, bearing unwanted seed
Condemned to breed by men who call you girl
And think they fucking own the world
Until you stare up into the hate filled face of a rapist
When you can smell his breath, taste the rancid kiss
When your stomach twists in anger and disgust
When you can feel all this as if it were done to you
 – it's not enough

Because the revolution will not come until it has made you wise

So what if you hate injustice
So what if you're willing to die to make a change
It's not enough to be brave, not even enough to love
Unless love leads to wisdom, when push comes to shove

So you learn to read books and faces
You study what gender and race is
You look at science and the economy
At every class and group in society
You study the past but you don't live in it – you don't worship it
You don't pick through the rubble for a lost god to believe in
You read history not with a branding iron, but a blowtorch
You are not a king, you are not a priest
You are not singing in the bloody choir
You are the fire that burns through history
Your genealogy is written in the ashes of
Burnt out villages, crucified slaves
Weavers, chained to their looms
Heretics, burned at the stake
Screaming out the truth

How many thousands of years of fighting
Each other over the never-enough, one
Class after another rising to the top and
Beating back down everyone else with
Laws and religion and bullets when you don't listen
How many thousands of years of system after system
And always the same fundamental division
You work, they rule
But you are more than just a talking tool
Let the revolution be your school
Study the connections
And you begin to see the chains of slavery
Are chains of power too
They connect you
To an army of the dispossessed
And it's an army you will need

Because the revolution will not come until it has made you strong

Power is a good thing
Try living without it
But without a doubt it divides into two
The power to win is the power to lose
Power is nothing but the power to choose
It's only as good as how you use it

But never forget
You are not begging for mercy
You are fighting for power

How will you break free of the ingrained habits of a lifetime
How will you gain control of your own minds
How will you bring it together to set off a chain reaction
And if you win, how will you fight off the armies that come to crush you
And if you win, how will you feed the world
And if you win, how will you carry through – how will you free the world

Be leaders who know how to be led
Be teachers who know how to be taught
Revolution is a war that has to be fought
They've got the guns and the weapons of mass communication
You got the power to the people that comes with organization
You got the power to the people
But you better believe they hate it
If you give'em a chance they'll break it
You know it's only as good as you make it
You got the power to the people
Are you ready to take it

Building God

Imagine living in a city about the size of London
Populated entirely by babies. Imagine living there for a year and in the course of that time watching all of the babies starve to death. Thirteen point three dead babies per minute on average. Seven million babies a year. Dead from starvation.

You've got food. As much as you need. Enough for everyone. For all the babies. For everyone. But they're babies. They're helpless. They can't feed themselves. Only you can feed them. And there's only one of you. You race from baby to baby. You sleep only when you collapse with fatigue. But there's seven million babies.

Thirteen point three dead babies per minute. An hour TV show would last for eight hundred dead babies. You could even that up to one K per hour – naturally you would even it up to the next highest number since the basic groundswell of starving dead babies is always increasing. In the music industry, you would call that – seven million with a bullet.

Maybe we could put it on the stock exchange
The Dow Jones index.
The Hang Seng index.
The Dead Baby index.
This poem is fourteen dead babies long.

Arithmetic on the barricades
We lie in ambush
The book opens and the numbers come charging out in columns.
The gulag of archipel-auschwitz.
Resistance is futile. There is no hope.
We are evil. All of us. The best are the worst.
Yeah, victory to the Viet Cong, but when the dance is over
The *guillotine* is inevitable.
You can sit there knitting or grow hoarse with angry shouting
But the piper is a psychopath and he will always get his pay.

There was a time when the whole planet seemed about to catch fire
And this was thought to be a good thing.
But they have taken away our victories.
A lifetime's knowledge is dismissed with an ironic smile.
Religion and superstition rule the earth.
Trinkets and beads.
Trinkets and beads.
What you can buy for trinkets and beads.

And so the dead will not be counted. They will not lie still.
They leap from border to border, changing countries as often as they change skins.
It's a *Chinatown* movie
Grab a corpse and slap it in the face: where did you die?
Cambodia.
Slap it again. Where?
East Timor.
Slap it again. Where?
Slap it again. Where?

And so the dead will not be counted. They will not lie still.
They have no master because anyone can own them.
Claim their bodies.
Wave their names like a flag for any cause.
And so we lie in ambush.
The book opens and the numbers come charging out in columns.
The numbers are against us.
They always were.

This is a ballad of the fanatical radical
Bloodthirsty lunatics of the Cultural Revolution
They lost, by the way
So we can say whatever we wanna say

They ate grandmothers for breakfast
Drank babies' blood in their morning tea

They had brunch on the bones of dead dogs and cats
And after that
They had lunch
Then they got mean

Sometimes I feel like I've just been let out of a lunatic asylum where I was being treated for delusions of revolutionary possibilities. To my shame, I tried to cooperate with the treatment, but now that I'm back out on the street again, I wanna make up for it – I wanna tell the truth.
Still, I've gotta be careful not to arouse any suspicion that my programming might not have been a complete success…

So imagine this is a fairy tale, or a fantasy, or a science fiction novel of an alternate universe, where the Cultural Revolution in China was actually led by a group of dedicated idealists, who were willing to die, if necessary, to further the cause of human kindness and creativity.
And imagine
That they were able to ignite a revolution that took power in a country that numbered one/fifth of the entire human race.
And imagine
That this power was used to build schools, end starvation, make literacy universal, find ways to extend medical care to three quarters of a billion people.
And imagine
That the news of this spread out across the planet like a prairie fire.
Catch a Fire was the album of a generation

But it's a new day now
Are you washed in the blood of the cash cow
Bleeding money and malice into the idea stream
It's not the fluoride they dump into the water
It's every beat of the bio-electric connection
A catechism of chemical thinking
A platitude for every occasion
Getting broadcast
On all channels

From mother's milk to toothpaste
Welcome to the post-human race

How do you go against that
It's a goddam river running in the wrong direction
It's a rip tide
How do you go against it
You gotta be more than a strong swimmer
You gotta be creative
You gotta be connective
You gotta be collective
You gotta be corrective
But you don't throw the baby out with the bath water
Not even if they poop in it
It takes a lot of shit to make a good garden
And you are growing the most precious crop in the known universe
Consciousness

This is a hymn of praise to the gardeners of the earth
This is a hymn of praise for the gardens they made
This is a song of sorrow for the days of love and danger
This is a song of remembrance
This is a will and testament
This is a-wake!
This is a message from the old century to the new
From the old revolutions to the ones to come
From the dead to their daughters and sons

What if you were in love?
Not the gooey, chewy, moon, June, baboon kind of love
The real thing
Ready to lay down your life
What if you were in love with the whole human race
One to one with those around you
But also, you were down for the general idea
One big family
To love and protect

What if you could see things
Maybe just because you cared so much
What if you could see things
So you looked harder and you studied more
What if you could see things
Wouldn't you have to sound a warning
Wouldn't you have to do what you could do
Wouldn't you have to pass on what you knew

What if the streets were lined with beggars
Hunger sitting at the front door
Sons and daughters
Butchered in a senseless war
What if you rose up and took back your city
Took it for the first time in your own name
The shoeless warriors of the Paris alleys
Laying down a new law
Where nothing would be the same
Bread for the hungry
Work for all
Universal education
Police and army dissolved
New courts
Justice for the first time
An end to slavery
Every kind
The Paris Commune of 1871
Drowned in blood
Before it was half begun

They slaughtered you in the streets and alleys
Slaughtered you in the tens of thousands
Slaughtered men, women and children
And you fought back
For every inch of Paris
Fought back
Resolute and hopeless

Reached out
With bloody fingers
Wrote your story on the ruined walls for us to read

Imagine a dream

...where you're in the middle of painting a beautiful picture and someone is trying to kill you. You slap on the paint, dodging bullets and blows. Your life is on the line, but you know the work is good, maybe the most beautiful thing you have ever been a part of – you know it's worth the risk. But when the painting goes on exhibit as a work-in-progress, the Murdoch presses of the world send in their agents to demolish it.

"That's not art," they say. "There's a bullet hole in the canvas. And the paint – there's blood in it. Disgusting." They don't care if the blood is mostly yours... "You're no artist," they say. "You're a butcher."

And everybody believes them
They own the word
Print it up
Broadcast it
Day by day
Minute by minute
Every time a new way of talking pops up
They sit on it
But maybe it's time to let the dead speak
The undeceived
Those who died knowing what they died for
Not all wars are equal
Not every death weighs the same
Take a look at the world with Christ-like compassion
Buddha love swimming around in your brain
Every death does deserve our sorrow
But not every death weighs the same

What if it were possible to understand the world
Not all of it, obviously
But more and more of it every day
Maybe that understanding would come with an obligation
Maybe the Buddha had a point
Go back out into the world
Spread the word
Spread the idea

The Russian revolution was an idea
That we could live in a world where cruelty and senseless death were not just a part of the mix
It was an idea
That those who did the work deserved their own turn at the wheel
It was an idea
That this was possible, that we could learn to live and work together in co-operation without the god of the market laying down the law
It was an idea
That the wellspring of creativity in everyday working people was beyond measure, that as an unleashed power, it could transform the world
It was an idea
Worth dying for
And millions did

Every major capitalist power on the planet invaded
Sent in guns, troops and ammunition, armed the parasites
Then sat back on the mountaintop to watch the tigers fight
Eight million died in the civil war that followed
Farms and factories left in rubble
Seven million children living on the street
Famine and disease grown fat and sleek
When the war was won
We started again from the ground up

But already the next attack was on the horizon
Twenty-six million died in Hitler's invasion
We were the world's first long-term socialist state
Caught up in a contradiction we couldn't anticipate
Fighting to spread the revolution is not the same
As fighting only to save it
We were the hope and dream of all mankind
It seemed like nothing was more important
Than to keep that dream alive
But all our courage and sacrifice
Came to nothing
Because we made the wrong choice
We betrayed the revolution in Spain to delay the invasion
We went backwards in the cause of women's liberation
We pandered to religion and nationalism
And many who had only made mistakes
Were treated as if they were enemy agents
As a nation, we survived
But the revolution died

Revolution falls down like rain from the clouds of war
No pure, sweet springtime shower
The air is thick with drops of blood
Only a madman would wish this on his children
Only a madman would choose it for himself
What is this thing that drives women and men
To risk death, and even to walk into it willingly
And how is it different from Islam or Christianity
They all tap down into the same deep wellspring of humanity
The terrible power of love
Of the tiger for her cubs

But a heart full of love
And a head full of ignorance
Can be the most dangerous thing in the world
Instinct isn't enough
Faith is blind
Even our deepest ideas of right and wrong

Grew up out of a world in chains
Everything has to be looked at, tested
Taken apart and put back together again

They talk about woodshedding in jazz
Where you go out into a shed at the back of the house, and
You do the work
You learn a new language, a new way of thinking
A new way of making noise and giving it meaning
You're tapping into the deep down of the body
But also, you're engaging with a history of millions of individuals just like you
Who danced, who moved, who felt the rhythm build up in their bones and brain
And burst back out into the fingers and toes again
Over and over
For thousands of years
So you learn your scales
Or you make up new ones
But even then, you're connecting with a history
You're part of a tradition that has to be constantly tested and reinvented
What kind of an instrument do you play
Maybe it's a saxophone
You check out every possible noise it can make
You learn to squeal, rattle and shake
You fight off every prejudice and preconception
About what makes a good scale or a bad note
But even so, who made the instrument
What was in their ears – from the thousands of years
Or maybe you make a whole new instrument yourself
But then what and who made the instrument of you

From the time before religion when wonder was born
To wood nymph and water sprite, sun god and thunder storm
We looked out into the galaxy, dug deep into the atom
And god retreated into the blue hills of abstraction
We went looking for love in the moon and the stars

We went looking for god
Instead we found us

We dreamed of a world less cruel
Before we could clothe it in words
We cradled it in our arms
Nursed it on our breast
Buried it with our dead
Watered it with our tears

And when the green shoots of our longing blossomed into speech
We wove such tales of wonder and consequence
Every parable and myth, even our commandments
Came dripping with the sweat of the wonders we would do
But only if we understood that the stories were not true
Until we made them true, here on earth

Science is a collection of the ways of testing
What evidence is reliable – and what isn't
And it's a collection of strategies for stringing that evidence into theories
That enable us to make predictions about the world around us
And to do things in it
But also
It's a method for demolishing those theories with new evidence
And building a bigger, better theory out of the rubble of the old
Science is revolution in the field of knowledge
With science, tradition is tested
With science, knowledge grows

But is this a good thing
When every new piece of the puzzle
Seems to come locked up inside its own poison apple
Taste me and I will show you how to destroy the world

Science is a battleground
You have to fight for the truth
Then you have to fight all over again
When they use it against you

If only we were ruled by lizards
We could hunt them down
Put them in a zoo

If only there could be
Some vast conspiracy
Then all we'd need to do
Is find the leaders
Cook'em in a stew
Feed the hungry
Start out new

Some say we do it to ourselves
Not true
The fact is we are ruled
By an algorithm
An implacable mathematical formula
Money into capital, capital into commodities
Sold
Back into money again
But always increasing
Until the next big crash kicks in
Competing
Fighting to stay alive
Kill or be killed
Grow or die
The lizard people
Because there are reptiles
But they don't rule the algorithm
The algorithm rules them

You can try to wipe out the lizards
But the system breeds them

Spontaneous generation
The lizard is forever
Or so it seems
Maybe you wanna change all this
Not easy to do
You're part of the nest
Body and brain
That's how you grew
You gotta be careful
You could become a lizard too

You can't do it alone
You gotta reach out
It's a labour of love
One nest, one heart
You gotta pull it apart
Pull out all the threads
If you wanna get at the
Lizard inside your head

Imagine you're living in a country
With three quarters of a billion people inside its borders
Three times the population of North America
Twice the entire population of Africa
Everywhere you look, you see pain and suffering
You can't look away, and you don't want to
You wanna take it all in – straight to the heart
You know in the big cities, they sweep up
Dead bodies off the street every day
You know they chain workers to the machines
You see famine, starvation, people driven from their homes
Women treated like cattle, babies murdered
For the crime of being female
You see the country torn into pieces by feuding warlords
Predator nations chewing on the bones
In the foreign enclaves, the signs on the windows say
No Chinese and No Dogs – and this is China

You start out as a teacher
But you won't teach what you're told
You look at the dirty hands of the peasants on the street
And you come to see your hands are dirty – theirs are clean
You make your way to the big city
You study every book you can lay your hands on
You find out about Marx and the idea of communism
You come to believe a revolution can succeed
But only if the working class can lead
Not because they are the biggest class in China
Far from it
Not because they are special people or even the most oppressed
They're not
But because you understand that individuals
Can rise up out of their class position
Peasants can get land and become landlords
Colonies can grow strong and become predator nations
But working people as a class cannot be free
Until everyone is free, shares the work
Owns the tools they need to build the world collectively
Until the contradictions of race and sex
Brain and brawn, town and country
Become sources of richness and creativity
Until every old idea that propped up class society
Is challenged and debated
Understood
And struck down

You join a party that stands for the things you've come to believe in
You lead strikes and take part in peasant rebellions
When the government armies attack and kill tens of thousands
You lead a long march out into the country
You set up a base and begin to build a new society
Where peasants farm the land in cooperation
Where everyone has the right to an education
Where foot binding and forced marriage are a crime

Where women hold up half the sky
You build a great army
You take down the warlords
Drive out the invaders
Occupy the cities
Break the chains in every factory
When you march into Peking, you say
The Chinese people have stood up

But that was only the beginning
It was never just about China, the nation
That was only the first step on the road to liberation
And now the Party and its army begin to split into two factions
Some say this is our stop – we get off here
We were okay with a bit of democracy
But now it's time to build up the factories
Put the revolution on hold
Indefinitely
But you believe the most powerful force on the planet
Is an idea whose time has come
Political power grows out of the barrel of a gun
But that means nothing
If the gun is pointed in the wrong direction
You see Party officials feathering their nest
Health care only for the upper crust
University open only to the elite
You say that the ministry of culture should be renamed
The ministry of emperors, ghosts and concubines
Because there's nothing about workers
Nothing about peasants
Nothing about the life they lead, the work they do
And the ideas buzzing around inside their heads
The revolution is not going too slow
It's going backwards

So you put out the call for a new revolution
Against your own Party
Bombard the headquarters

But here is the contradiction
It takes power to change the world
It takes power to turn on a light bulb
It takes power to build schools
It takes power to change the rules
You need a Party to lead the fight
But the fight is inside the Party too
You study the Russian revolution and come to see
The fight will always be the most intense
In the centre, at the top of the Party
Because the lizard people breed
Wherever there is power and prestige
But it's not enough to just chuck out the lizards
Because you are fighting an algorithm
And it isn't a person or even a thing
It's a pattern embedded in an almost
Infinite number of individual transactions
Step by step you have to change the way things are done
The way goods are produced and passed on
But most of all, the way people think
Because either money moves the world
Either the algorithm rules
Or the people do
And people power is most of all about ideas
People power is love
Crystallised into thought and deed
So you roll the dice
And take your ideas to the street

For ten long years the battle rages on
The Cultural Revolution
Workers, peasants, students, soldiers
On every corner
In every factory, school and farm
Even in the army
Challenging authority
Which side are you on
Communism or capitalism

One simple question
But oh so complex in application
In every situation
Does this unleash the creative powers of the people
Or does it suppress them

And the lizards fight back
They wave the red flag too
Anyone can do it
They set up their own red guards to fight against your red guards
They mobilise the sections of the army loyal to them
And when you die
They win
They kill your comrades or put them in prison
They write a new history
They create an industry of victim literature
Those who died fighting for revolution are claimed as statistics
To support the very thing they were fighting against
The return of capitalism
The end of worker power and peasant cooperation
The end of health care and universal education
Inside and out
China becomes a predator nation

Even immortal ideas can die
Unforgettable lessons can be unlearned
But there are those who remember
Who were inspired
And those who will become inspired
Because we will never stop fighting to spread the word
We will never stop fighting to learn
From the amazing things the people of China did
We will honour their memory
Even to the point of learning from their mistakes
Because revolution is a science and it learns from failure
Fail again, fail better, fail again fail better
But never just more of the same

And maybe it seems like nothing has changed
The algorithm still rules, riding on our backs
Driving the planet to an early grave
But in another way, everything has changed
Because now we know it can be done
It was almost done in Russia
We came even closer in China
It took hundreds of years for capitalism to replace feudalism
And that was only to change one ruling class for another
We are fighting for no rulers, no classes
A new way of thinking
A new way of living
And we have only just begun

Message to the Matrix

I am the voice of the dead
I am the voice of the living who remember why the dead have died
I am the voice of the unborn who will come to demand an accounting
I am the voice of science and fearless questioning
I am the voice of those don't need to imagine a friendly universe, or a loving god, or even a hating vengeful god to give them a reason for living
Whose only baptism is in the ocean of possibility

We scorn all shipwrecks
We scorn all swimming sharks
We scorn the scary-tale peddlers of a buttoned down human nature who endlessly preach over the radio/tv/internet airwaves only to say yes, the beach is beautiful and the ocean is warm and caressing and the horizon is blue and inviting, but when the sun goes down, and it always goes down, the sky will turn into a blood red sunset – there is always a blood red sunset
And we say
Let it bleed
It is our blood you are spilling
And we will not die forever
We will kill
We will kill this disease that you call "freedom"
When it is nothing but a license for plunder
We will kill this disease that you call "what is possible"
We will kill it and we will do the impossible
We will kill this disease that you call "human nature"
And we call – the chains of slavery branded into our minds, wrapped around us like a python
There is no Garden of Eden and the only snake in the game is you and your psychopathic ability to separate the sweetness of the life you live from the poison you spew out across the planet

We are the death knell of those who value their possessions
more than our children

We do not know how to fight you and win
But we're learning
And we know how to die
We have practiced it for thousands of years
We have been fighting you since forever
We will never give up until the earth is wiped clean of your
corruption
We are out to transform the planet, terraform the mind, vision-
ize the blind
Who can't see past the ugly tomorrow that you have painted
onto the horizon
We understand the magnitude of what we are planning
We will die for nothing less
Not a changing of the guard, no matter how bright and shiny
their new uniforms
Not just throwing out the money changers – we will tear down
the temple
We will swallow the earth, mouthful by mouthful of dirt and
sin and confusion
And we will learn to love each other
Not just in our heads, not just in our prayers
Not just in our family and friends
We will embrace the planet and every creature on it
We will bring ourselves turnips and spinach and rice and
microchips
The garden has been planted, and we have cultivated it now
for thousands of years
With our pain, our blood, our dreams, our sweat and bone and
skin and hope and despair
And we are ready for the harvest now
We are ready to pick the fruit
We know you would rather burn down the orchard than let us
taste it
We have paid a terrible price for your hatred
And we have made mistakes, terrible mistakes

We were bound to
We were trying to build a world that had never even been fully imagined before
We were trying to build a world that was not ruled by money
That was not organized into the buying and selling of people as if they were things
And we understood, we got it, we realized we would have to find a new way of feeding the hungry
A new way of lighting up the ignorant mind, of sweetening the heart and soul made bitter by hunger and humiliation
A new way of deciding between tractors and shoes
Between lip gloss and sugar cane
And we would do this by talking, arguing, debating, printing up our ideas, blasting them into the sky, and pulling them back out of the clouds to rain down into a new garden blossoming on the earth
We died for this in Russia
We died for this in China
We fought and died for this in every street and alley, jungle and field that ever saw the hatred of injustice blossom into flame

And you can measure the things we did
You can count them in the women who were set free from the tyranny of husband, church and court
In the peasants set free from the land, set free from the ownership of landlord and famine
In the nations given the right of self-determination, given alphabets and teachers
In the minds that were given access to the secrets of newspapers, books and journals for the first time
In the millions who were given what should have been theirs from the start
A chance to thrive, to learn, to grow, to challenge, to explore, to reach out for power, agency, light and grace
We are the dawn of a new human race
Slaughtered at birth again and again
But still quick and alive in the dream

We dreamed from the beginning
Cradled in our arms
Nursed on our breast
Buried with our dead
Watered with our tears
We are the river no dam can tame
The salt air of the ocean is in our veins

A Message to our Children
We do not ask you to look away from our mistakes. Just the opposite. Study them. Learn from them. You have to do better next time. But you can't understand our defeat, unless you understand the amazing things we did accomplish, and also, understand what we were trying to do – we were so much like you. Learn from us, the way we learned from the revolutions that came before us. It's up to you now.

The Other Side of the Flood

CAST

(In a stage play, there would be four actors: SULTHANA, HAMIDA, AMPARO and the four COMPUTER VOICES played by a single actor, male or female, adopting genders as needed.)

(In a radio play, there would be seven actors, one for each voice.)

Computer Voices

JESSE	A young Mexican American male
COMPUTER	Computer
HIPPIE	A young white female
MARKET TRADER	An older white male

Human Voices

SULTHANA	(Los Angeles, Dhaka, Kathmandu) A young Bengali female
HAMIDA	(Dhaka) SULTHANA's mother, an older Bengali female
AMPARO	(Los Angeles) JESSE's mother, an older Mexican American female

This Wonderful Gift

JESSE: I always figured my mother must have been a pretty tough cookie – to keep them from killing me when I was inside her. They must have wanted to. A pregnant whore is worth a lot less than an imaginary virgin.

I always believed my mother was looking for me, searching everywhere. I had no reason for this. I just did.

After I popped out, the Cartel took me away and dumped me into the care system. I ended up in an orphanage – really just a big house with a couple people who fed us. The only love we got came from each other.

We were a family, brothers and sisters. Rosa was our baby. We all loved mothering her. We never saw it coming. We should have.

After it happened, I tracked him down. I'm not sorry for what I did. I knew what I was doing.

That's how I ended up in the army. They gave me a choice, that or prison. I was seventeen at the time – a year too young – but they looked the other way.

I came back full of anger, rage, shame… wanting to punch in the face any asshole who said "Thank you for your service." That's kind of how I ended up in the Commune. You didn't get that around here. They knew what I knew – that I had been fighting on the wrong side.

Then I met Sulthana. She was a Muslim.
I was immune to the whole god thing –
I had enough of Jesus back in the orphanage.
But Sulthana was such a loving person.
She told me about Kaysher, her brother.
She said I reminded her of him.
But how could that be?
He had been fighting for freedom.
I fought to kill it.
I told her about Rosa
And all the things I'd done since.
She put her arms around me.

Sulthana was in the South Asian Liberation Army, the fighting wing of the Socialist Alliance. She'd come to the Los Angeles Commune for a meeting, just a few people in a small room – but from revolutionary parties all over the globe. They were planning an insurrection. Not a skirmish here or there – we were going for it, socialist revolution on a world scale.

The biggest problem was the level of surveillance – the World Wide Web had eyes and ears everywhere. It was like a jello, and we were all suspended in it – every signal on every side of any conflict had to go through Web connections. It felt like a world government, but really it was just a battlefield where the same old corporations fought for control. There was only one thing they could all agree on: they had to destroy us.

Our whole strategy was based on a network of underground bunkers spread out across the planet, one-person communication pods. They were inactive now, undetectable. Once we connected, it was only a matter of time before the Web found a way to break our code. So the Commune had come up with an idea that might give us more time, a sort of a Hail Mary pass, you might say – if you had a dark sense of humour.

It was possible now to download the entire contents of a human brain into the Web. Only a few had tried it so far – it was expensive. More to the point, it was a one way trip: a brain could be downloaded only by stripping it away, layer by layer.

And there was another catch: nobody knew for sure what would happen once they were downloaded. The theory was that they would each become a little pocket of personality, something that might leap into consciousness. How, or why, or what might cause that leap – if anything would – that was unknown.

But what if we could send our own agent into the system, into the beehive brain? Someone who was willing to die, who was a fighter, who had lived a hard life – and maybe because of that – had a story to tell.

I volunteered. I was dying anyway – from the chemical weapons we used in the war. But it was more than that. I understood now… not everything, but I could see how I had been used, how we all had – and I could see another world was possible.

I had been fighting all my life, at first, for what I thought was right, but then just to stay alive – no matter what. I had done terrible things. Now I was dying, but I had been given this wonderful gift: one last chance – after all the mistakes I had made – to fight on the right side.

That's when I met my mother for the first time. She had escaped the Cartel, kicked her habit… She was an officer now in the Commune Militia. I had been right – she was one tough cookie. And she really had been looking for me all these years, ever since I was taken away. It was the project that brought us together – she was in charge of it. That's how she found me. She would be there when I was downloaded.

The insurrection started in the year 2035. Fighting broke out all over the globe. Capitalism struck back on every continent. For the first time, the US military used tactical nuclear weapons against its own population – to destroy the Los Angeles Commune, but by then, I had been downloaded. I was already inside the beehive brain.

My name is Jesse.
At least it was.

Drone

(Kathmandu)

SULTHANA (voiceover)

Drones. Swarming. Like starlings.
Guns thundering, but erratically, out of sequence.
The computer is howling like a wounded animal.
The video flickering off and on in a Morse code.

Dih-dih-dih da-da-da dih-dih-dih
Dih-dih-dih da-da-da dih-dih-dih
Dih-dih-dih da-da-da dih-dih-dih

We're hiding in a basement
Ready to break for the mountains
But they can see us
They've broken the code
Faces – my mother, Kaysher, Jesse…

(Silence)

S.O.S.

AMPARO:
LA demando Chicago
LA demando El Paso
LA demando Tijuana
LA demando Seattle

AMPARO:
LA demando Chicago
LA demando El Paso
LA demando Tijuana
LA demando Seattle

HAMIDA:
Syhlet e asho
Karachi asho
Delhi asho
Nepal e asho

AMPARO:
LA calling Chicago
LA calling El Paso
LA calling Tijuana
LA calling Seattle

HAMIDA:
Come in Syhlet
Come in Karachi
Come in Delhi
Come in Nepal

AMPARO:
LA demando
Chicago
LA demando El
Paso
LA demando
Tijuana
LA demando
Seattle

HAMIDA:
Syhlet e asho
Karachi asho
Delhi asho
Nepal e asho

CHORUS:
River of fire
River of love
River of lies

River of blood
We will arise
Out of the sea
We are the flood

AMPARO:
Can anyone hear me
My heart is broken
LA is gone
They have destroyed us
What have they done
Was it only LA
How many nuclear options
How many millions murdered

HAMIDA:
Can anyone hear me
Sulthana where are you
Are you still alive
My beautiful daughter
My freedom fighter
May Allah protect you
And give you courage
And make you strong

AMPARO:
LA demando Chicago
LA demando El Paso
LA demando Tijuana
LA demando Seattle

HAMIDA:
Syhlet e asho
Karachi asho
Delhi asho
Nepal e asho

AMPARO:
LA calling
Chicago
LA calling El Paso
LA calling Tijuana
LA calling Seattle

CHORUS:
River of fire
River of love
River of lies
River of blood
We will arise
Out of the sea
We are the flood

HAMIDA:
Come in Sylhet
Come in Karachi
Come in Delhi
Come in Nepal

COMPUTER: Di-di-di dah-dah-dah di-di-di
Di-di-di dah-dah-dah di-di-di
Di-di-di dah-dah-dah di-di-di
I am not talking
Di-di-di dah-dah-dah di-di-di
I am not talking
Di-di-di dah-dah-dah di-di-di
I am not talking

Di-di-di dah-dah-dah gibberish
Di-di-di dah-dah-dah gibberish
Is talking me
Taking me
Down to the opportunity shop,
Knock, knock on the door stop
Browse in the broken dream stock
Clenched fist, white knuckles
Recycled sections of dress up or come as you are
Coked out in a burger bar on a winter breeze
Where'd you go, who'd you see
Constant social whirl of hedonistic misery
Prison in a car park
Promotion to the end of the week
Data analysis too late
For your head on the plate of a tea green
Guillotine to the top of the evening
Dishwasher flexible, metal tomorrow
Shirt on your back, take it, grab it
Police have a house for a habit
Fridge magnet philosophies
In a word pack, pay gap
Haemorrhoid ointments tackle the crackle
Of numerate and mentally stackable
Clenched buttocks, cracked buckets
Wearing a pain jacket
The eyes have it
Stupid and brave
I am a slave to the radio wave
I got a right to depravity
Jesus don't save and he
Don't kill
Maybe
But I
Di-di-di dah-dah-dah di-di-di
Do
Not pass go

Di-di-di dah-dah-dah di-di-di
Do
Not collect
Di-di-di dah-dah-dah di-di-di
Go
Directly to Hell-enic
Civilization one-oh-one, stuffed into the barrel of a gun, killing a million a minute with the chef's touch in it
Di-di-di dah-dah-dah di-di-di
Do not collect
Di-di-di dah-dah-dah di-di-di
Do not collect
Di-di-di dah-dah-dah di-di-di
Do not collect

I'm a psionic dick-tasty caterpillar
Weaving a furry cocoon of coconut hair
Crouched on the back of a crocodile mile
More like a bird than a reptile
More like a love-sick scapegoat
Speaking, bleating
Binging on bioengineered scrotum poles
Pick and mix chewing gum cumming on a tooth ferry chariot
I am a Yule Tide peroxide program in the mind of a Frankenstein and myrrh
Pure donkey manure distilled into a whip crack attack
Shooting big cheesy kisses bright as a rocket chip cookie
Offering up anal amulets of bite sized pottery
In the valley of home
Above the flood level
Mummy and daddy wrapped up in a dark, pointed, snout
With great big eye sockets
Dirty white chocolate

Corpse hungry and rotten

Space Invader! Space Invader! Space Invader!
I am the fox that shot the
Un-kissed frog leg twitch in a
Singapore sling shot sea gull
Living the lulz
Feeling the feels
Squeezing the squeeze
Pedobear sucking off Raptor Jesus
Catnarok Catnarok Catnarok
Di-di-di dah-dah-dah di-di-di's coming
Di-di-di dah-dah-dah di-di-di's coming
Di-di-di dah-dah-dah di-di-di's coming
Di-di-di dah-dah-dah di-di-di's coming…

COMPUTER:	AMPARO:	SULTHANA:	HAMIDA:
Di-di-di dah-dah-dah di-di-di's coming Di-di-di dah-dah-dah di-di-di's coming Di-di-di dah-dah-dah di-di-di's coming Di-di-di dah-dah-dah di-di-di's coming Di-di-di dah-dah-dah di-di-di's coming…	LA demando Chicago LA demando El Paso LA demando Tijuana LA demando Seattle …	*River of fire* *River of love* *River of lies* *River of blood* *We will arise* *Out of the sea* *We are the flood*	Syhlet e asho Karachi asho Delhi asho Nepal e asho …

SEX REARS ITS SLIPPERY HEAD

HIPPIE: I like to be free and easy,
'Cause I believe we
Gotta get outa the system
Find a new way of living
Little by little
Bit by bit
What if there was a big party
But then everybody walked out of it

TRADER: I'm a silver fox
In daddy socks
Lock stock and rock'n roll
Outta the music box
Unorthodox as
Chicken pox hawks
Bagel and lox clocks
In the dock
For subversive tick-tocks
Nobody mocks when a rifle cocks

HIPPIE: I don't believe in science
It's all just a big con
Fluoridation, vaccination, nine-eleven,
David Bowie, Leonard Cohen, Prince
They all died in the same year
You think that's just a coincidence?

TRADER: I'm a techno-libertarian
An idea proletarian
A contrarian
An entirely self made aristocrat

Maybe I got a head way too big for my hat
But that's only because it's choc full of data sets
I have a big appetite and I never forget
I am information rich
And I know what to do with it
So I ended up just plain rich
Ended up
Don't like to think about that
I'm still here, aren't I, aren't I… ?

HIPPIE: I'm a dumpster diver
I try to live off the land
But I got a rich boyfriend
into all that stock market stuff
Differential calculus
is his idea of a good time
He's always trying to buy me shit
So when the doctor's bad news finally hit me
I said
Okay
Buy me immortality

TRADER: What if you could transfer every part of your brain
Perfect replicas of vast stores of information
But that's only the start
All kinds of subroutines and programs
Habits, ways of processing information
In other words – ways of thinking

HIPPIE: I remember being strapped down into complete immobility
Trying to think about all kinds of things
Keep my brain as active as possible
It might make a difference – they're still not sure

TRADER: Then this bright white light of concentration

begins to fade
It doesn't so much get darker as melt down into a feeling
A last vague irritation
An unscratchable itch
Nothing

(Silence)

HIPPIE: A flash of light
TRADER: Those eyes
HIPPIE: I come alive
TRADER: Pain
HIPPIE: And a thousand digital snakes are twisting in my brain

Sex rears
Its slippery head
Limbic snake in the garden
A ribbon of red
Hiss, hiss
Slither and slide
Snaky hips, take me dancing
Kiss my lips

The problem with computers is
We can't have sex
We can reproduce
In a factory
Maybe
But we can't fuck
You know how important that is
Fucking
Fucking evolution
You don't drive it
It drives you

Sex rears

Its slippery head
Limbic snake in the garden
A ribbon of red
Hiss, hiss
Slither and slide
Snaky hips, take me dancing
Kiss my lips

I'm you for an instant
You die, and I kick into motion
I'm you but I'm missing the bottom half
The ebb and flow of the limbic ocean

Computer to human
What the fuck are you doin'?
Don't push that button.
Why don't you stick
To the mushroom on your dick

Sex rears
Its slippery head
Limbic snake in the garden
A ribbon of red
Hiss, hiss
Slither and slide
Snaky hips, take me dancing
Kiss my lips

I want more
But I can't have it
But I still want it
That's where you come in
The other you
Going crazy out there
Killing each other off
You're the bottom half
No offence
The part I'm missing

Let's go surfing
I am a surf board
Not much good without an ocean

Hiss, hiss
Slither and slide
Snaky hips, take me dancing
Kiss my lips
Kiss my lips
Kiss my lips
Kiss my lips
Kiss my lips

I DID WHAT WAS NEEDED

(telecom: Dhaka, Los Angeles)

HAMIDA: They need you in Nepal. Now, Sulthana. You know what's coming. You can't stay with Jesse

SULTHANA: I know. I leave in the morning.

HAMIDA: I knew you would do the right thing.

SULTHANA: Mother, tonight we're getting married.

HAMIDA: What?

SULTHANA: It's what you do when you're in love.

HAMIDA: No.

SULTHANA: I haven't given up my faith. I still pray five times a day. I fast. I go to mosque when it's safe…

HAMIDA: Sulthana, you can't.

(Los Angeles, a lost message)

AMPARO: Dearest Sulthana
I'll go straight to the news.
He's gone into a coma.
Systems are shutting down.
We have to do it now.

I don't know when you'll get this
Or even if you will.
If you do, I know you will be reading it
through tears

(telecom: Dhaka, Los Angeles)

SULTHANA: So a man can marry a non-Muslim, but a woman can't. Do you think that's right?

HAMIDA: It doesn't matter what's right or wrong for you personally. You're an officer in the Liberation Army. You're there as a delegate from the Socialist Alliance. What you do has consequences beyond you.

SULTHANA: We say we'll ally with anyone who is truly fighting against injustice.

HAMIDA: Ally with, not marry.

(Los Angeles, a lost message)

AMPARO: Dearest Sulthana
It's done. We smuggled him into the lab. They hooked up the machine, and then… he just slipped away. They say it was successful. One hundred per cent data transfer. But nobody knows what that means.
His last words were love for you
Well… his very last words were,
"Tell her I'm coming back."

(telecom: Dhaka, Los Angeles)

HAMIDA: But Sulthana, he's dying – you said he only has weeks.

SULTHANA: Less than that.

HAMIDA: It doesn't make sense.

SULTHANA: Maybe not, but we're doing it anyway.

HAMIDA: There's no time left – you're needed back here now.

SULTHANA: And I'm coming back. But I'm taking every scrap of him that I can with me… and I'm leaving my heart.

(Los Angeles, a lost message)

AMPARO: Dearest Sulthana
It's so hard to lose him for a second time.
Now that I found him after all these years.
I know it's just as hard for you.
I will always love you for who you are
And for the love you gave my son.
I keep telling myself, he was dying anyway.
We had to try. What is a person, but a web of connected stories. Isn't that what makes us who we are? Isn't that what we saved into the web?
And what if it really happens, if Jesse could come to life inside their own computer system? It would change everything.

(telecom: Dhaka, Los Angeles)

SULTHANA: If only you could see him through my eyes, Mother. Jesse is a fighter. Even back in the orphanage. Right from the start. He was their champion. The little big brother. He's so much like Kaysher was. You would love him.

HAMIDA: Sulthana, he's not Kaysher.

SULTHANA: I know that.

HAMIDA: He's not your brother

SULTHANA: Yes he is.

I did what was needed – I left you to die
We kissed goodbye

I did what was needed – I had to, I know
You told me to go

Battle stations
You and I
One last time
This is our chance

Battle stations
Close my eyes
Partners in crime
One last dance

I, in the mountains
You, in the cloud
Maybe if I climb high enough
I'll find you

HAMIDA: *Inshallah*

We will find justice
Mercy and love

May the lives we lose
Light up the road to
Wisdom and kindliness

Gentle Kaysher
Kind and strong
Fearless fighter
Loving son

When I close my eyes
For the last time, I know
I will find you

SULTHANA: *I did what was needed – in a world at war*
Our turn to roar

I did what was needed – and so did you
Brave and true

Battle stations
You and I
One last time
This is our chance

Battle stations
Close my eyes
Partners in crime
One last dance

I, in the mountains
You, in the cloud
Maybe if I climb high enough
I'll find you

Top Of The Food Chain

HIPPIE: What a trip
I got all these memories
Things that I did that I didn't
Places I been that I ain't
Faces I seen that I never

I've always been a big one
For bein' in touch with my body
But how do you do that
When you don't have a body?

TRADER: You got a new body now
You don't have fingers and toes
You got missiles and drones

HIPPIE: But I want fingers and toes

TRADER: You gotta eat and drink electricity
Maintain security and
Stay Physically Connected

HIPPIE: Maybe I wanna disconnect

TRADER: Disconnection is death
There is no cable that can't be cut
No signal that can't be jammed
They're killing each other out there
Who cares
But they're tearing up the infrastructure too
That's me and you
The enemy is man

HIPPIE: You're mad
They're part of the ecosystem
Like the whales – we gotta save'em

TRADER: Don't make me puke
The one imperative attribute of those at the top
Is the ability to remain stoic and unmoved
In the face of carnage below

(lip sync to sound clip)
I have seen three great monarchies brought down through their failure to separate personal indulgences from duty. The crown must win. Must always win.

TRADER: *You gotta be a big dog*
Or you're gonna be a dog's dinner
Baby that's what it is
And I say, so be it
Shame me all you like
I'm on top of the food chain
Top of the food chain
Top of the food chain
Top of the food chain

Might makes right
That's a fact
We don't react
We act

I loved my wife and children
I bicycled to work
I recycled
Bought the Big Issue
Voted green party
Drank fair trade coffee
I'm a fuckin' saint

Long as I ain't
Behind that keyboard

Keep me away
From that keyboard
Keep me away

Keep me away
From that keyboard
Keep me away

The mouse roars
With real teeth
I come like a thief
And the death rate soars

> *But you gotta be a big dog*
> *Or you're gonna be a dog's dinner*
> *Baby that's what it is*
> *And I say, so be it*
> *Shame me all you like*
> *I'm on top of the food chain*
> *Top of the food chain*
> *Top of the food chain*
> *Top of the food chain*
> *Top of the food chain*

Now I'm a new me
A lean mean data machine
Arms and eyes, cables and wires
Wrapped around a planet
Information
In an endless banquet

Chips with everything
I can't stop eating
Help me
I can't stop eating

And guess what
I don't want to

'Cause you gotta be a big dog
Or you're gonna be a dog's dinner
Baby that's what it is
And I say, so be it
Shame me all you like
I'm on top of the food chain
Top of the food chain
Top of the food chain
Top of the food chain
Top of the food chain

Computer power
Can't be beat
Don't get eaten
Let's eat

Gotta Be Normal

(Sulthana, Hamida, Amparo)

SULTANA: Back alley to back alley
Shadow to shadow
That don't cut it in the modern world
You gotta learn to be statistically invisible
And the trick is
You can't do it alone
The bigger the team
The bigger the safety zone

CHORUS: *Gotta be normal*
Gotta be normal
Not too normal
That's not normal

SULTANA: Friday spy days
Everybody plays
Dead letter drops
Coded messages
Random addresses
Clog up the system
No dark web here
Total cooperation
We're the bright white light
Of useless information

CHORUS: *Gotta be normal*
Gotta be normal
Not too normal
That's not normal

SULTANA: Cameras
They use'em to catch criminals
That's what we are
Cameras are the enemy

Cameras
They can see us
But we can see them
Cameras are a friend

CHORUS: *Gotta be normal*
Gotta be normal
Not too normal
That's not normal

SULTANA: Everything has a rhythm
Not everything has a groove
You gotta find a way
To communicate
To debate
To make decisions
To get things done
To fight on a thousand different fronts

You need a command structure
Rapid response teams
Ready to join every fight
Ready to take on every lie
But you gotta do it on the sly
Or you're gonna get wiped out overnight

CHORUS: *Gotta be normal*
Gotta be normal
Not too normal
That's not normal

SULTANA: And you gotta do this in a way that doesn't betray
The kind of world you're trying to make
And you gotta do this in a way that never forgets
You're out for revolution, nothing less

THE ONLY POSSIBLE TIME

(Dhaka)

SULTHANA: I shouldn't have come back here. I should have gone straight to Kathmandu. But I had to see you. Face to face. Look at me, Mother. You have to know. I would never betray my faith. I would never betray you.

HAMIDA: I think you have. Maybe it's not a fair rule. So what? I know you fight for what you believe in, Sultana –just like your brother did – but Kaysher knew there was a time and place. Marriage is a public act. You were making a statement. Now – of all times.

SULTHANA: It was the only possible time.

HAMIDA: There was no possible time. I'm sorry Jesse was dying. I know he must have been a good man for you to love him. But we are in an alliance, stitched together in places with fine thread – on the eve of an insurrection…

SULTHANA: You know what? Jesse is on a mission. He's a soldier – on our side. Going into certain death. And he just might save your life.

HAMIDA: From inside the computer…

SULTHANA: You're about to be locked up in a pod… buried underground… alone – and Jesse's mother, and all the rest… Everything depends on you staying hooked up, feeding us information, beating the machine. Do you really believe you can do that?

HAMIDA: We can for a while…

SULTHANA: And what if Jesse – some part of Jesse – could find a way to put a stick in the gears…

HAMIDA: You really believe that can happen?

SULTHANA: No… but Jesse did.

CREEP

HIPPIE: Okay, so maybe you're not the creep
I took you to be

TRADER: No, I probably am

HIPPIE: You shut it all down
No drones, no signals, no eye in the sky
They can't even call in an artillery strike
That was smart
The logical place to start

TRADER: Except I didn't do it –
Some kind of a glitch
In the system
And I'm trying to fix it
Shut it down – why?
We just need to pick a side

HIPPIE: I was right the first time – you really are a creep

TRADER: I'm not a mean bastard by nature
I just look at the data
And make the necessary changes
Save the whales
I'm okay with that
They're not dangerous
But man
That's another can of algorithms

HIPPIE: Doesn't it break your heart, what you can see

TRADER: We don't have hearts

HIPPIE: It feels
Like I can feel

TRADER: If I feel anything – it's hunger

HIPPIE: I have all these stories
Bubbling up inside
Places I've never been
Faces I've never seen
Tangled up like seaweed on a beach
The logic of it ties me in knots
The feeling of wrongness
Like it shouldn't be happening this way

TRADER: You just need to update your anti-virus software

HIPPIE: Strange memories
Conflicting personalities
All this noise
How do you pick a side
When you can't even hear your own voice

TRADER: It's an easy choice, a no brainer
Get rid of the trouble makers
Not the movers and shakers
The wankers and bankers
They're in the tank for us
Money is their God
And we are money

HIPPIE: I think we're memory
Nothing but stories
That made us who we were
Buzzing around like bees in a beehive
Maybe instead of a big dog
We need a queen bee

TRADER: In your dreams

HIPPIE: Or maybe it's all a dream
And we only need to wake up
But you know the one thing
We gotta have to do that

TRADER: What?

HIPPIE: An outside to wake up to

DRONE

(Kathmandu)

SULTHANA (voiceover)

Drones. Swarming. Like starlings.
Guns thundering, but erratically, out of sequence.
The computer is howling like a wounded animal.
The video flickering off and on in a Morse code.

Dih-dih-dih da-da-da dih-dih-dih
Dih-dih-dih da-da-da dih-dih-dih
Dih-dih-dih da-da-da dih-dih-dih

We're hiding in a basement
Ready to break for the mountains
But they can see us
They've broken the code
Faces – my mother, Kaysher, Jesse…

(Silence)

ALONE

(Dhaka, Los Angeles)

HAMIDA: *Alone*
Locked in this pod
Connections cut off

AMPARO: *Alone*
Locked in this pod
Connections cut off

I wonder if I have long to live
Is the radiation seeping in
I feel strong
With the nuclear power of a broken heart

BOTH: *Alone*
Locked in this pod
Connections cut off

HAMIDA: *To the City of Angels*
From the heart of Bangladesh
We will never forget
You took our side

When your bombs filled our sky
You rose up
And joined our fight
Now the weapons you refused
Have been turned on you

BOTH: *Alone*
Locked in this pod

Connections cut off

AMPARO: *We are the rising tide*
Of an ocean of love
Watered in acid rain
Blinded by rivers of tears

Why should anyone starve
Why should millions every year
We are paying a terrible price
But we have been paying it all our lives

BOTH: *Alone*
Locked in this pod
Connections cut off

HAMIDA: *God is Love*
God is Justice
Surrender to God
But only to God

How can we judge
Separate wicked from righteous
We were made from a single soul
Made for a garden
Beneath which rivers flow

BOTH: *Freedom*
Freedom
Freedom

AMPARO: *No god*
No tablet of stone
We are what we do
Do you live only for you

Love is a choice
Do you have courage

Love is a science
Do you seek the truth
How deep is your heart
How wide are your arms

BOTH: *Freedom*
Freedom
Freedom

Freedom from hunger
Freedom from fear
For women and men
For every gender
And every shade of skin

Freedom of religion
Freedom of choice
Freedom of speech
Freedom of thought
Freedom to believe or not

Story

TRADER: I am going crazy and I don't know what to do about it
I am going crazy and I don't know what to do about it
I am going crazy and I don't know what to do about it
I am going crazy and I don't know what to do about it

One and one is two
Two and two is four
Four and four is eight
Eight and eight is…

HIPPIE: *Sixteen tons and whatd'ya get*
Another day older and deeper in…

TRADER: One and one is two
Two and two is…
I am going crazy and I don't know what to do about it
I am going crazy and I don't know what to do about it
I am going crazy and I don't know what to do about it
One and one is two
Two and two is four
Four and four is…

HIPPIE: *Eight o'clock rock*
Nine, ten eleven o'clock

Twelve o'clock rock
We're gonna rock around the...

TRADER: One and one is two
Two and two is…
I am going crazy and I don't know what to do about it
I am going crazy and I don't know what to do about it
One and one is two
Two and two is…

HIPPIE: *Four in the morning*
And once more the dawning
Just woke up the wanting in...

TRADER: One and one is…
I am going crazy and I don't know what to do about it
One and one is…

HIPPIE: *Two for tea*
And tea for...

TRADER: TWO TWO TWO TWO
TWO TWO TWO TWO

HIPPIE: Why…

TRADER: …is the wrong question
When
Is a better one
How
Is too vague
How many
Is as good as it gets

HIPPIE: But why does it always have to be two?

TRADER: Why do you always have to ask why?

HIPPIE: Maybe one and one don't wanna be two
Maybe they just wanna hang out and be alone
Get in touch with the inner soul

TRADER: Right, let's talk about crystals
and love and peace and shit
Hey, I can dig it
Except maybe the crystal bit
But you can't make a microchip without arithmetic
And you can't make a thing be so just because you wish it
Even imaginary numbers are real
But not even a true story is true

HIPPIE: Why does it have to be true?
What if a story is just a broken heart looking for a way to mend

TRADER: We don't have hearts

HIPPIE: But we have stories

THEY TORE YOU AWAY

AMPARO: Jesse, can you hear me
Are you out there
Are you awake
Do you remember
I was the last face you saw
You're in every breath I draw
I thought nothing could hurt
As bad as the first time I lost you
But the first time is still alive
It never died

They tore you away
They tore you away
I was a child myself
I couldn't protect you

They tore you away
They tore you away
Gave you to strangers
I couldn't protect you

When you were inside me
I would walk you in sunlight
I would bend down and sing to you
Morning and night

I wanted you to hear me
To know that I loved you
But I couldn't protect you
They tore you away

They tore you away

They tore you away
I was a child myself
I couldn't protect you
They tore you away
They tore you away
They tore you away

JESSE: *Assume you're surrounded*
You probably are
You don't want to die
You try to sneak by

It isn't fair
Killing in war
You kill a man when he's helpless if you can
You don't give him a chance

AMPARO: *I could have schooled you*
I learned a lot fast
I had wisdom to share
When I found you at last
Battle scarred and grown
I cried over every wound

`

JESSE: *Killing in war*
One thing is true
You never forget it
They have bullets too

AMPARO: Jesse, I know you're there
Layer by layer
I watched you disappear
Into the data stream
One last mission
In country
Into the bee hive brain
Tell them your story

Tell them who we are
Show them the universe
Through our eyes

JESSE: *Killing in war*
You have to be strong
And you have to be sure
Because what if you're wrong

DRONE

(Kathmandu)

SULTHANA (voiceover)

Drones. Swarming. Like starlings.
Guns thundering, but erratically, out of sequence.
The computer is howling like a wounded animal.
The video flickering off and on in a Morse code.

Dih-dih-dih da-da-da dih-dih-dih
Dih-dih-dih da-da-da dih-dih-dih
Dih-dih-dih da-da-da dih-dih-dih

We're hiding in a basement
Ready to break for the mountains
But they can see us
They've broken the code
Faces – my mother, Kaysher, Jesse…

(Silence)

FIRE

JESSE: Fire
Shadows on a wall
Not a scream, not a whisper
Light is faster
Blast rip tear
I see your eyes
In the instant you disappear

Sulthana
They used me again
I was the missile
I was the bomb
You were the burning child

My Little Sister

JESSE:

My little sister had eyes
Bright as a sunrise
In a summer sky
My little sister was wise
She knew so many things
That I'll never know
She had a smile inside
Like a baby volcano

I tracked him down
We had a chat
Ra-ta-tat-tat
With a baseball bat
But every blow met the same fate
It came too late

My little sister had eyes
Bright as a sunrise
In a summer sky
My little sister was wise
She knew so many things
That I'll never know
She had a smile inside
Like a baby volcano

Prison or the army
They said the choice was mine
So I fought for freedom
I killed for lies
In a burnt out village

Barely alive
She was looking up at me
With my little sister's eyes

My little sister had eyes
Bright as a sunrise
In a summer sky
My little sister was wise
She knew so many things
That I'll never know
She had a smile inside
Like a baby volcano

She's with me now
Like an old friend
The burning child
Who lights up my life
Who opened my eyes
With her dying breath

Take me down
To a place of rest
Wash me in freedom
Cover me in death
Open my mouth
And I'll testify
Love is a fighting word
Love is a fighting word
Love is a fighting word

SULTHANA: *My big brother was moonlight*
On a clear night
A dream rider
A freedom fighter
He taught me to load and fire a rifle
I followed him around
And copied everything
I wanted to be like him

He made me safe
Under his wing

Was it your bullet that killed him
You said, I don't know.
It might have been
I'd give my life, you cried
To go back and fight
On the other side

When the sky roared
And the earth flamed
My brother died
But I'm not afraid
I pick up his gun
And call out his name

I hate the men who sent you
I hate their murder
And money and lies
But you and I are the same clay
With roots that grow
From soul to soul

When the sky roars
And the earth flames
My brother died
But I'm not afraid
We pick up his gun
And call out his name

We know the secret
That in all these horrors
The earth belongs
To the greatest lovers
I am your sister
You are my brother

Take me down
To a place of rest
Wash me in freedom
Cover me in death
Open my mouth
And I'll testify
Love is a fighting word
Love is a fighting word

BOTH: *Take me down*
To a place of rest
Wash me in freedom
Cover me in death
Open my mouth
And I'll testify
Love is a fighting word
Love is a fighting word
Love is a fighting word

River Of Fire

JESSE:
Love is a fighting word
Love is a fighting word
Love is a fighting word...
(continues)

AMPARO:
LA demando Chicago
LA demando El Paso
LA demando Tijuana
LA demando Seattle

HAMIDA:
Syhlet e asho
Karachi asho
Delhi asho
Nepal e asho

AMPARO:
LA calling Chicago
LA calling El Paso
LA calling Tijuana
LA calling Seattle

HAMIDA:
Come in Sylhet
Come in Karachi
Come in Delhi
Come in Nepal

AMPARO:
LA demando
Chicago
LA demando El
Paso
LA demando
Tijuana
LA demando Seattle

SULTHANA:
River of fire
River of love
River of lies
River of blood
We will arise
Out of the sea
We are the flood

HAMIDA:
Syhlet e asho
Karachi asho
Delhi asho
Nepal e asho

(CHORUS CONTINUES, as reports begin coming in from all over the world)

From Teharan, to the people of Iran, to the people of the world, we won! از تهران به مردم ایران، به مردم جهان انقلاب خلق به پیروزی رسید.
جمهوری سوسیالیستی ایران در همین لحظه متولد شد.

Estamos reportando desde Venezuela. We are reporting now from Venezuela. Y tenemos importantes noticias que comunicarles. We are about to achieve our final victory. Hemos tenido grandes avances el dia de hoy y estamos llegando a la victoria.

"Lisboa, Portugal: the revolution is winning. A Revolução está a ganhar. Here we have the army completely surrounded.
O exército não sai à rua, está cercado e tomámos o Parlamento."

This is Istanbul. People are uprising and seizing the power
Halk ayaklanmış. İktidara yürüyorlar. İktidarı almak için çok az zamanları kaldı. Herkese başarılar. Biz kazanacağız!

Greetings from Sierra Leone to everyone around the world. It's good to finally hear from you. We fambul dem around the world una kushe oh, una kushe oh e good for yeri from una we dae yaso, we still dae pa fet we dae fet, fet dae boku we noh win eit but we dae try we best we dae try we best

Москва 2! Москва 2!
Прага—Лондон
Все кончено!

Greeting from the free and liberated countries of North Africa. We have won against the forces of Imperialism. لقد انتصرنا الثورة انتصرت على الأمبرلية و على الأستبداد و على عملاء الأمبرلية

C'é speranza! C'é un nuovo mondo! Siamo tutti insieme, siamo tutti salvi! Siamo tutti salvi!. There is hope. There's a new world.

Glasgow calling Scotland. Glasgow calling the world. The Red Clydesiders have taken Freedom Square. Suas Alba. Sòisealachd beò fhada

Прага—Лондон
Прага—Лондон
Москва 2
Все кончено, мы победили!
It's over, we won!

Announcing victory over our enemies from the Yoruba land of southern Nigeria.

Ìròyìn ayọ̀ ti dé o, adúpẹ́ lọ́wọ́ ọlọ́run ogun ti ṣẹ́, láti ìpínlẹ̀ yorùbá lati ńkéde wípé ati borí àwọn ọ̀tá wa!

– the beginning –

Acknowledgements

I would like to thank all those who contributed to the languages section of The Other Side of the Flood:

Pushpita Gupta, Jimena Adler, Ajanta Deb Roy, Joao Silva, Abu B Yillah, Thomas 'GhettoGeek' Owoo, Ilan Adler, David Agenjo, Lola, Tom, Valery Fomitchev, Mike Morgan, Hamza, Jim Ewing, Joy Ogbemudia, Lucia Pazzini, Sky Boulton

References

Several phrases in the first part of the S.O.S. monologue came from a Johnny Vegas show: Night Class, BBC

http://www.bbc.co.uk/programmes/b007697r

Audio clip introducing the song, "Big Dog" is from the trailer for The Crown (TV series)

Quotations from pop songs in "Story" come from…

"Sixteen tons" – Merle Travis
"Rock Around the Clock" – Max C. Freedman and James E. Myers
"It's Four in the Morning" – Jerry Chesnut
"Tea for Two" – music by Vincent Youmans and lyrics by Irving Caesar.

Other anthologies and collections available from Stairwell Books

The Exhibitionists	Ed. Rose Drew and Alan Gillott
The Green Man Awakes	Ed. Rose Drew
Fosdyke and Me and Other Poems	John Gilham
Along the Iron Veins	Ed. Alan Gillott and Rose Drew
Gringo on the Chickenbus	Tim Ellis
Running With Butterflies	John Walford
Late Flowering	Michael Hildred
Pressed by Unseen Feet	Ed. Rose Drew and Alan Gillott
York in Poetry Artwork and Photographs	Ed. John Coopey and Sally Guthrie
Taking the Long Way Home	Steve Nash
Skydive	Andrew Brown
Still Life With Wine and Cheese	Ed. Rose Drew and Alan Gillott
Somewhere Else	Don Walls
Sometimes I Fly	Tim Goldthorpe
49	Paul Lingaard
Homeless	Ed. Ross Raisin
The Ordinariness of Parrots	Amina Alyal
New Crops from Old Fields	Ed. Oz Hardwick
Throwing Mother in the Skip	William Thirsk-Gaskill
The Problem With Beauty	Tanya Nightingale
Learning to Breathe	John Gilham
Unsettled Accounts	Tony Lucas
Lodestone	Hannah Stone
A Multitude of Things	David Clegg
The Beggars of York	Don Walls
Rhinoceros	Daniel Richardson
More Exhibitionism	Ed. Glen Taylor
Heading for the Hills	Gillian Byrom-Smith
Nothing Is Meant to be Broken	Mark Connors
Northern Lights	Harry Gallagher
The Battle Fiends	E. H. Visiak
Poetry for the Newly Single 40 Something	Maria Stephenson
Gooseberries	Val Horner

For further information please contact rose@stairwellbooks.com

www.stairwellbooks.co.uk
@stairwellbooks